IN

HOURS

Rescue Press, Iowa City
Copyright © 2015 Marc Rahe
All rights reserved
Printed in the United States of America
First Edition
ISBN: 978-0-9885873-9-7

Design by Sevy Perez
Text set in Stratum2 and FF Tisa
rescuepress.co

ON HOURS

Marc Rahe

THREE

For Leigh

ONE

SUMMER COLD

There was a sickness in me.
It was not serious but enough

to stay home. The sickness was a thing
in the world and then it was me. I was

eggs and bacon and
what our forefathers did. There was a way

to avoid this but this
is what I got. Reality

television and drums on the radio.
The day went on for barely a while.

By the time it was over I saw
I could have done more.

THE CLOUD OF PROMISE

Lifting herself and almost dropping forward
the rabbit forages.

I call Leigh to the window and touch
her back while we watch. We admire

the high alertness of rabbit ears
and the quick chewing. We imagine

what multitasking is. Steam rises
from our coffee. Inside,

the air is still sky.
The door is closed. There is

no door. From our coffee,
the dark cloud rises. Dry

ground is hard to shovel.
On consecutive days, we have each

killed a spider in the shower.
The neighbor has a manual mower

to push past his garden.
This cloud is promising.

UNVEIL TO BLUE

Dark cloud, you are going
away and you didn't give.
Mine is not the only want,

not the deepest or most
hollow call. Dark cloud,
we want you to, don't you

want you to? The land is dry
and you withhold. Weeds
grow tall in our longing.

Mine is but a renter's wish
but for the fields,
for the markets won't you?

It would be your end but not
forever. Every
blade has gratitude.

THE RIGHT TOOL FOR THE RIGHT JOB

The snow shovel can be used in summer

if you are one who cannot bend far,
whose arms do not straighten,
whose arthritic fingers cannot be made to reach

the ground without the whole body
following. If the body dropped
is unable to rise unaided.

There is a key to open your door.

The key, dropped, unreachable there,
must be retrieved. The snow shovel can be used to
scoop the key, to lift it. If the snow shovel

is held close, the key can be grasped.
The shovel is replaced, the door is unlocked.
Enter your home. Examine your shame.

ON SELF-CONSCIOUSNESS

A man with a beard without
a beard looks nothing like

himself.

Clean-shaven, I am living history.

LOCAL HISTORY

A long-closed rail station. Across
the street, drink specials at The Club Car.
The building of the Iowa Avenue bridge

followed a vibrant ferry business.
To go west more easily.
It was raining but not on our side

of the street. That wasn't the most
embarrassing day, but I think
of it as at the same time. One thing

follows the next: gratitude
follows nudity, for instance,
a towel after streaking in the storm.

So much for wine and cherries—
she reminisced on certain
afternoons as condensation

dripped from bottles in light
softened by the blinds. The punch
line redeems the set-up,

life continues after lives, summer
after summer, until the swimming hole
is deemed unsafe and closed.

ON SILENCE

I can't help wanting
not to say anything
wrong on the occasion
of someone's suffering.
I touch
a shoulder and ask,
"Is this the spot?"

I look up just when
the muted documentary
is showing bodies
on a Civil War field,
and think, *those must
not be real bodies.*

I turn up
the volume and learn even
the soundtrack contains silence.

Silence is contained
in the nonverbal vocalizations
of the person with cerebral palsy
indicating a need only
someone who knows her would

understand.

SUMMER CLOTHES

When you spit on
the sidewalk, it is a victory
for glistening,

as reflective sunglasses
mirror nature.
Some people are paralyzed

and have voluntary muscle
control of only their eyes.
With their gaze—and the right

communication partner—
a pane of lettered glass between them—
they can spell

entire books into the world.
I recycle but I could do
without mosquitoes.

April showers
can last for hours. Make
your gaze your

alphabet—on what street
do you make your list? How
often do you garden? What

do you like about this library?

DOWN

the tub drain,
the disposal, down
in the kitchen
garbage bag,
the microcosmic
crawl and flagellate
in fecundity
rich as the garden

where wild onion
has taken over,
spread even beyond
the sidewalk. Their
slender stalks topped
with life-treasure
the bees bother
in the sunlight,
in the humid

and pungent air.

While my fan oscillates.

While my sweaty chest is bare of you.

PARKING LOT

It is from here, parked behind
this rental house complex,

that she sees a rabbit race
from dark to dark across

the headlights and says,
"Look at that rabbit." The communal lawn

displays a wading pool, a swing set, and an orange
and purple plastic truck. We look

at the rabbit though the rabbit
is long gone or just out

of the observable, outside the insistence
of light in front of the parked

and air-conditioned vehicle
on the cracked, littered,

and weedy lot while wars wage on the station.
The rabbit is gone out of sight and into the imagined

world and actual rest
and a good chance of not being eaten

and how loud must the neighbor be to be
heard addressing her grievance

to her friend who is just now departing
her porch? Possession

after possession
hurled into the red glow.

THERE IS NO PAIN

There were more than three
weeks until the longest day
of the year. An eclipse

occurred. A friend had died
and another friend
was dying. We took
a picnic and a shadow
board. To look without

looking. An animal made
a call, or a growl, a kind
of lowing, or
a growl in the trees.
It was nearly sunset.

When a cloud passed,
we thought we'd missed
our chance to see.
A pinhole aperture
functions as a lens.

I saw stained glass.
A door that opened
to the lot. There is no pain
to warn when
the retina starts to burn.

FROG POND

This scissored-out
face in

the photograph
I pinch

in the mirror
edge. I

admit
starving I

have called
myself in

in spite of
trees, reclining.

ON DISTRACTION

What is our undoing if not
hunger? The smell of dish soap

a hope against what rises
from the bowls left soaking

in the humid dark.
It is the middle of summer,

the nights are getting longer.
Outside, midday by the fountain,

children cool
despite the sun. Here

in the library, two friends talk
just loudly enough for some

of their words to be misfit from
the background noise. It was

never my intention to listen,
to let what attention I have

away.

TWO

ON VULNERABILITY

While the rotini's water boils,

you scratch your calf
and note how

the tree's leaves illustrate
the breeze. Even diamonds are

flammable. The ring of the electric
burner is brown with orange in it.

You turn a fan on.
On the linoleum, you are

careful in your socks.
What are the leaves

showing you?
Only glass

keeps that branch out.

CONFINES

Bodies I have shared have become immortal;
in the shade of two trees hangs an equation of insects.

MAN AT BASEBALL GAME, ALONE

Fans and spectators relax.

Peanut shells and wax paper contribute,

crunching and clinging. You come alone;

you find your father here
in the cup beneath your seat,
in the popcorn under your soles.

Crews clean up after.

It's okay. Everyone here
is more or less at peace.

You watch

a boy in the concession line
wrap his hands in his shirt. The tangle
of cotton in his hands.
The cuffs

of the father
are the return of a hand to your face.
The ballpark is the place

where he never bruised you.

Everyone yells, everyone spills
trash. You came here to find
something gentle.

LIVE BIRTH

Hold the flashlight to your finger.
The red of danger exists in your hand.
Your inner snakes, your rats,
flush your wrist.

Hold the flashlight to your armpit.
The red does not go so deep
as to discern from the vermin tails,
the snake bodies coiled almost
as one body, or the lung
in its relentless motion.

This is not the heart,
nor a place in the heart.
The twist friction is your
only furnace. It heats your
content to make through
vasculature to the farthest

surface of your form.
Almost free, your content
learns all it can
stand of the lessons of cold.

Take between the jaws of pliers
one of your toenails. The application
of force could remove
choice from your content.

ON RESPONSIBILITY

Someone will be angry in the house
until they fall asleep. How can
approval be gifted? Snow hasn't
covered the tips of the grass.
The taste of your own salt.

A cardinal is on the feeder. Streets
are aligned with the cardinal directions.
All walking is walking in place.
Before, the song of a cricket

in the night. At dawn,
don't you resent the alarm?

POSTCARD

The building filled with smoke and foam.
The night street—wet.
Lights of another city beneath its surface.

Further below were new stars,
new constellations.
What shore did they show?

The building was emptied of people
before the walls collapsed,
making the graffiti a puzzle.
Some of the people left.
One postcard

shows a photo of faces browsing
bookshelves in a ruined building.
Faces I have touched.
Vessels that will never return.

THE MAJOR PORTION OF ALL LIVING THINGS

You dropped a coin down there.

Your pockets were heavy as an udder.
Even now your pants grow aquatic,

host a library of alien life.

To imagine is to rush down there
reckless. On an icy surface,

walk like a penguin,

with safety. When you put
your ear on your ear you can hear

the strokes your blood has learned

to navigate the canals of your skull.
Above the coral, our octopus

flattens its tentacles, changes its colors

to suggest another creature.

YOU WERE OF A CLOUD

Out of a gray sky rain plucks
its loneliness. Nothing can make

it hear me as it pelts the glass.
Over my pelt, I am sweatered.

I know from the street, light is warm
and framed by my and my

neighbors' windows.
Under the eaves is a rut worn

into the ground by years of rains
since before I began my renting.

I know rain is pouring down there
in a curtain. I can hear it.

It is cold and dirty. But, rain,
you are new. You were of a cloud,

then the wind took you every way
by solitary drops. A greater

force drew the whole time.
You were of the sky then you arrived

from the sky to my home on the outside.
Even in that muddy hole you

welcome the other rain coming after,
as though you weren't yet a stranger.

THE SUN, THE MOON, THE STARS

Across the field near the school
a teacher spread objects to illustrate scale.

An acorn here, a child there.
Called the child "sun" and how far away

the acorn must be to be
our planet. Could it

be seen there at that distance
to give a glimmer of distance?

The grass and grasshoppers,
the wind and the sound in it

must be given to be nothing
in the model. Nothing

must be held in mind
that holds the world.

THE END OF YEAR QUESTIONS ARE ALWAYS VERY HARD

I must tell you that I just got
my hair cut, and may have
found a barber that I like.

I'm still reading
cereal boxes. This solitude

feels like retreat.
Maybe I shouldn't have left.
Maybe once I find

work, shame will cease to be
my companion. Some time,
some change. I can see

poverty from here. You asked
if I'm seeing any pretty girls—
I see them everywhere.

AGAIN THIS YEAR

When I see the commercial for the summer
beer, it is not yet even summer.
It is unseasonably
hot. The rain keeps coming

and the chives are overtaking the flower
bed I think of as not my flower bed
with its smell. I used to think it was
coming from the garbage
cans until I was told. I keep
to myself, but I'm here
a lot. I could tell you stories.

DON'T KNOW WHAT A SLIDE RULE IS FOR

When I boil water to cook
for myself, the idea of *a better
kitchen* doesn't usually occur.

If I had you over I'd want you
not to notice
how much recycling is under

my table, pizza boxes making
a shelf over many empty cans.
You are at work waiting

for the clock to let you go.
Sometimes I am so compelled
by a video game that I lose
weight. There is only one voice through
the wall: my neighbor's complaining

tone into her phone, muffled
sounds. A pot in the trash,
filled with soil and a dead plant.

Over the long term,
I could make it on eggs and oatmeal.

ON STABILITY AND SECURITY

Always I check the coffee maker twice
to see that the ON light is off.

I do not know the renter
of the other half of this house,

what hazard her habits might bring.
One morning I heard nested in the birdsong

the chirp of a smoke detector sounding
every minute or so.

HOW TO LAST

The day died on the couch.
The leaves of the birch nearly white

as the sun goes down.
To discern imagination from memory

the time traveler marks
X on the time-map.

A devil was discovered in a cloud
after centuries. A dog lifted its paw.

To be thrown a stick, or
to be thrown a bone.

I could never make proof
from the given.

I take my jacket
because I need its help.

THREE

THE RABBIT

Of course I knew the rifle.
My ears that knew
the announcements of each
flake of January knew
all cracks of the air.

My nose knew the smells
that came before
and after the shots. I
could hardly be found
in my modest coat.

My racers could never
catch. Ground I left
was their only prize.

I was swift, I eluded and

left more children than
you'd think. Sometimes I would
see myself in a kit's watchful eye.

A thousand deaths
I must have avoided.
A hundred thoughts must
have been my friend
until one tore through
and revealed
the sky.

TO FIRST WORLD PROBLEM SOLVE

Mechanical production of the re-.
Given the problem of X,
solve for *the solution is more*.
To solve for potential, cock
the hammer. Double the number
of finger bones of a child's hand—
a flight of shirts. Oh sunlight,
there are so many weeds, yet

you won't ignite the sky.
Therefore, is is is is an argument
to feel gratitude for what one
does not have to have. Wings
in the ear—air compressions
of metronomes, dripping ceilings.

OFFICES

Trees all along

the streets. Sometimes on a long ride,
I wish for the transporter to get
without in-betweens. It must be

abysmal: the distance between
her itch and the quadriplegic's
hand. Not all wheelchairs are made

equally well-suited for being fastened
down for transit, she instructed me.
If the pain in your bone is a pavement

through hard freezes,
place that on the scale approaching
ten in an office the color of dirty bone.

To scale, the earth sets a standard
of smoothness beyond the measure
of a ball bearing. I think of a long enough

lever. I set myself in the printer's place.
Three-hole punch is an option, a benefit
from the work of strangers in the past.

A younger maple has smoother bark.
The black carpet stain was a walnut shell
squirrel-shredded on my walk.

My house seems filthier when I dust.
I am falling. I should watch my step.

FIXED

I am the windows
that look out on windows.

I am the gaze. I am the unreal

bodies behind the drapes.

Mine is the black counter
wiped down again and again.

I am a caretaker;
I worry from afar.

I worry a sore.

Where
do you go, after?

Between privacies is the dark
of a key-filled lock.

From inside my gem my look

is hidden, each face
familiar when facing away.

SHORE

Here were stones for a citizen,
a member, that sat before
an absence that is counted,
an absence that is counted on,
and shore was not precise,
was an invitation for precision
out of some lens, some narrowing lens.

IN DIRECTIONS THEY CARRY THEIR HEALTH

On the edges of the city, cornfields.
Where you sit, a philodendron growing under
florescent lights. There is no street.

There are mannered gestures.
There is a preview on the screen
of a video game with zombie jesters.

The room is impressively clean
but you make no comment.
Those people aren't here now.

You have two hands, a back.
You have closed a lot of doors
and are thinking of a back door.

CLOTHES MAKE THE MAN

The weekend is almost over.
It is cloudy, mid-afternoon
and the laundry in the dryer
will soon be ready

for Monday morning.
Outside, a squirrel grips
with its hind paws a snowy
branch of the juniper bush

while with its front paws it pulls
the wire mesh of the swinging bird feeder.
It chews and hangs suspended
before dashing down the branch.

Some birds return, though none I could name.
Where is a blue jay, or cardinal?
My clothes are still wet and,
for now, it is warm by the dryer.

INANIMATE ALLIES

When I am not alone

outside my home, on a street
all is wave and object.

Sometimes footsteps

are in my footsteps from behind
like a potential lie, but an extra

shadow can be cast on the ground
before me in warning.

With a lamp-post at my back,
my footsteps circle me, detecting.

Sometimes insects

are air vibrating and invisible—
a glass jar of grass and twigs,

holes where air could pass oblivious

and prolong a contained flicker.
Sometimes an unlit window

can mirror a stranger closing.

ON CROWDS

I get a haircut, but it grows.
Past the cheerleaders'

float where youth waves.
The bank is closed anyway.
Who took the metal from the earth

to make so many staples? Who
has shorn the sheep?

Want can also be need.
I want to stand outside

an establishment and say, "Hi,"
to my friends or people I know

as they walk out. I like to smile
at a stranger. It is good
if they smile back. It is good

if they drop their hand from
their cleavage, good of them

to keep me. Some animals have
horns that curve backwards.
Occasionally when I follow a curve,

my shadow leads.

"A" FOR EFFORT

Day, you bring me the siren
held in your morning air.

I am grateful to be
inconsequential. Makers

of spell check, I was never
competent. It is the voice in

the error that speaks
to me.

I am not even

in this I. Aspirin,
with your extra eye

lend me peace.

THANKSGIVING

I cut a few pieces ready to eat.
What's left is uncut but not whole.

I wash and stack. Luck and grip
are factors in what I feel.
These are the dishes of the dead.

I forget. In that upstairs was
a push-button light switch. A childhood

fascination with cause—the white ON
pops out when the black OFF is in.

Part of the floor is a hatch.

THE HUNGRY

I could feed you. I rest the channel.
Now it's your story.

Due to my recliner, I have a huge mouth
that precedes me in dream. There was

an entrance and now a complex of hallways,
late papers, a haunting by a class

I failed years ago. There was an entrance
and I entered—a fresh haircut, my mother's

spit on my face where toothpaste had been.
There had been flies on your lips on the screen

but that was before and in a place outside.
I would risk your infection for an exit.

Locked out of leaving, the clock is steady.
There is a space on the table where initials

have not been carved. Between us
is a workbook filled with blanks.

BROKEN BRANCH

All day you lean over
the river under the weight

of early ice, still leafy

and unprepared. Before midnight
you'll splinter and drop.

Joining your shadow, you'll float.

Free of the shore, you'll think first
that shores pass, too—backward rivers.

Something true all along,
but you'd never guessed.

The sky there, pushing as usual,
and the river pulling like a root.

ACKNOWLEDGEMENTS

Many thanks to the editors of the journals in which some of these poems, or earlier versions, first appeared: *Ink Node*, *iO: A Journal of New American Poetry*, *jubilat*, *notnostrums*, *Paper Street*, *PEN Poetry Series*, *Petri Press*, and *Prompt Press*.

BIOGRAPHY

Marc Rahe is the author of *The Smaller Half* (Rescue Press, 2010). His poems have appeared in *iO: A Journal of New American Poetry*, *jubilat*, *notnostrums*, *PEN Poetry Series*, *Petri Press*, and elsewhere. He is a graduate of the Iowa Writers' Workshop. He lives in Iowa City and works for a human service agency.

RESCUE PRESS